Marguerite Productions in association with
Theatre Royal Haymarket Company, Bob Boyett, Horipro and Umeda Arts T
present

Ruthie Henshall Julian Ovenden Alexander Hanson

A NEW MUSICAL
MARGUERITE

Music by
Michel Legrand

Book by
Alain Boublil/Claude-Michel Schönberg/Jonathan Kent

Lyrics by
Herbert Kretzmer

Original French Lyrics by
Alain Boublil

Annalene Beechey   Mark Carroll   Keiron Crook   Matt Cross   James Doherty   Siubhan Harrison
Jon-Paul Hevey   Joanna Loxton   Jessica Martin   Julia J. Nagle   Amanda Sim   Duncan Smith   Gay Soper
Lincoln Stone   Phillip Sutton   Simon Thomas   Andrew C. Wadsworth   Lucy Williamson

Associate Producers
John McColgan and Moya Doherty   Debra Black   Stephanie P. McClelland
John O'Boyle   Ricky Stevens   Robert G. Bartner   Jamie deRoy

Casting Director	Production Manager	General Management
Pippa Ailion	Dominic Fraser	Act Productions

Orchestrations and Arrangements by Michel Legrand and Seann Alderking

Musical Supervisor	Musical Director	Video and Projection Designer
Seann Alderking	John Rigby	Sven Ortel

Lighting Designer	Sound Designer
Mark Henderson	Paul Groothuis

Choreographer	Musical Staging /Additional Choreography
Arthur Pita	Nikki Woollaston

Designer	Directed by
Paul Brown	Jonathan Kent

ALAN BOUBLIL OVERSEAS LIMITED

&
WISE PUBLICATIONS
PART OF THE MUSIC SALES GROUP
London / New York / Paris / Sydney / Copenhagen / Berlin / Madrid / Tokyo

COME ONE, COME ALL 9
JAZZ TIME 14
CHINA DOLL 19
THE FACE I SEE 23
WAITING 31
INTOXICATION 34
DAY BY DAY 38
I AM HERE 44
DREAMS, SHINING DREAMS 48
I HATE THE VERY THOUGHT OF WOMEN 53
THE LETTER 60
WHAT'S LEFT OF LOVE? 63
HOW DID I GET TO WHERE I AM? 68
FINALE 73

COME ONE, COME ALL

Music by
Michel Legrand

Lyrics by
Alain Boublil/Herbert Kretzmer

JAZZ TIME

Music by
Michel Legrand
Lyrics by
Alain Boublil/Herbert Kretzmer

CHINA DOLL

Music by
Michel Legrand
Lyrics by
Alain Boublil/Herbert Kretzmer

THE FACE I SEE

Music by
Michel Legrand
Lyrics by
Alain Boublil/Herbert Kretzmer

WAITING

Music by
Michel Legrand
Lyrics by
Alain Boublil/Herbert Kretzmer

INTOXICATION

Music by
Michel Legrand
Lyrics by
Alain Boublil/Herbert Kretzmer

© Copyright 2008 Bouberg Music Limited and City Lights Productions Limited.
Administered for the United Kingdom & the Republic of Ireland by Alain Boublil Overseas Limited.
Administered for the USA by Alain Boublil Music Limited (ASCAP) c/o Joel Faden & Company Incorporated.
All Rights Reserved. International Copyright Secured.

This hal-lu-ci-na-tion, cra-zy and ob-sessed. This fas-ci-na-tion will not let me rest. She pressed her lips to mine and she in-tox-i-ca-ted me!

DAY BY DAY

Music by
Michel Legrand
Lyrics by
Alain Boublil/Herbert Kretzmer

1. Day by day, there is a time when men must choose;
2. Day by day, peo-ple are van-ish-ing from sight;

clear the land, clean it at last!
sud-den-ly no-bod-y there!

© Copyright 2008 Bouberg Music Limited and City Lights Productions Limited.
Administered for the United Kingdom & the Republic of Ireland by Alain Boublil Overseas Limited.
Administered for the USA by Alain Boublil Music Limited (ASCAP) c/o Joel Faden & Company Incorporated.
All Rights Reserved. International Copyright Secured.

Day by day, clean out the rabble and the Jews;
Who's to say where they are taken dead of night?
3. Day by day, look at the queues out on the street;

root 'em out, rub 'em out fast!
Never ask, never ask where!
look at 'em standing in line!

Make them pay, punish the guilty for their crimes;
We're alive, Germany conquers in the east;
We're okay, plenty of booze and lots to eat:

make 'em all, make 'em all hurt!
Germany marching ahead!
caviare, big cigar, wine!

Here we'll stay, tak-ing ad-van-tage of the times;
We sur-vive, Ger-ma-ny saves us from the Beast;
Let them say these are the days of our de-feat;

let 'em eat, let 'em eat dirt!
Sta-lin-grad count-ing her
look at us do-ing jus'

dead!

fine!

4. Day by day, there is a change a-cross the land;
5. Day by day, there is a shift-ing of the sand;

1.
we will go where the wind blows!

2.
blows! We will turn when the wind

turns! 6. Day by day, many a
7. Day by day, people are

French-man's going to fall; round 'em up, make 'em all
ask-ing what we did; sav-ing Jews, that's what we

41

Em
pay!
did!
Em D/E Em D/E
Down they go, spill-ing their
Yes, we say, we were the
4
4
C/E D/E C/E D/E
guts a - gainst a wall;
he - roes of the day;
C/E Bm/E
hun-dreds will suf - fer this
ev - 'ry day sav - ing a
Em
day!
Yid!
4
4
Am G/A Am G/A
Yes - ter - day, Ger - ma - ny
Hip, hoo - ray! Wel-come the
F/A G/A F/A G/A
stood here at our side,
Brit - ish and the Yanks!
F/A Em/A
ab - so - lute, res - o - lute,
We were here fight-ing for

43

I AM HERE

Music by
Michel Legrand
Lyrics by
Alain Boublil/Herbert Kretzmer

I've told myself to stay away, perhaps a hundred times a day. I've tried to shut my eyes, but still I see you ev'ry-

-where; you won't disappear. Armand, it's happening so fast. I'm throwing caution to the wind. It seems so clear, I know now where I am at last. I am here, what happens now is yours to say. I am

here to take, or spurn, or turn a-way. It's ab-surd, and yet I'm not too proud to say I will go, I will stay; say the word, I'll o-bey. Time was when they all came knock-ing at my door; face-less men who knew my price and knew the score. Let the past be the past, let it go. I'm standing here before your eyes; standing here without a mask, without disguise. Look and see, Armand, I am here.

DREAMS, SHINING DREAMS

Music by
Michel Legrand
Lyrics by
Alain Boublil/Herbert Kretzmer

MARGUERITE: Young, still so young, he sleeps now without a care. How

© Copyright 2008 Bouberg Music Limited and City Lights Productions Limited.
Administered for the United Kingdom & the Republic of Ireland by Alain Boublil Overseas Limited.
Administered for the USA by Alain Boublil Music Limited (ASCAP) c/o Joel Faden & Company Incorporated.
All Rights Reserved. International Copyright Secured.

48

little does he know of me. You and I to - geth - er,

safe to - geth - er we lie and reach for

ARMAND
(MAR.)
Dreams! How I dreamed! I dreamed we could soar like ea - gles.
dreams.

In my sleep we leap the sky, you and I to -

-geth-er. Close to heav-en we fly. In the shad-ow of the night we take wing, in the fad-ing of the light. An-gels sing in the beat-ing of our hearts. When I look in-to your face, I am strong; in the hold of your em-

C7/G
A/F
ARMAND
Dm/F
A7/E
-brace, I be - long. In the hur - ry of the day, you are
Dm
G9
F/C
C
(MAR.)
In the shad - ows of the night then you ap - pear. Has there ev - er been a
(ARM.)
near. And so we dream our dreams, fool - ish dreams. Im -
f
B♭/D
F/C
Bm7♭5
F/C
time quite like this? Can there ev - er come a time not like this? So we dream on while we
-ag - ine a world just start - ing here in the fad - ing of the light.

may, take our chanc-es day by day. In our lit-tle share of heav-en we'll dream.

We dream our dreams.

ARMAND
Dream, do you dream? What se-crets d'you hide in sleep? Per-haps you dream of oth-er arms, oth-er lips to rouse you. I watch you there, and I could weep.

I HATE THE VERY THOUGHT OF WOMEN

Music by
Michel Legrand
Lyrics by
Alain Boublil/Herbert Kretzmer

D♭5 N.C.
I've known them, ev - 'ry sort of wo - man; I've seen their greed, I
♩. = 69
B♭m7 E♭9sus4 A♭maj7 D♭9sus4
know their guile. Some - where to - night in some bed - room she
3 3 3
G♭maj7 B9sus4 Emaj7 N.C. A♭7sus2/4
Freely
N.C.
lies, shin - ing with sweat with a boy be - tween her thighs. She
♩ = 138
D♭add9 A♭7sus4
fills his mouth with kiss - es. I hate her for the shame in - side me, this se - cret shame that

haunts the night: the dog with-out a name in-side me, the dog that begs and soon may bite. Who am I to this wo-man? No bet-ter nor worse than a pas-sing ac--quain-tance who puts cash in her purse. She was all that I want-ed, she meant

Par - is to me. I have al - ways loved Par - is, now I hate what I see!

♩ = 138

I've served the state, I've done my du - ty; I won't go hun - gry at this feast. I hun - ger for her mouth, her beau - ty; let beau - ty come and feed the beast! How I hate all these Frenchmen: whores, wastrels and Jews! How they flaunted their splendour, how they whine now they lose! Give the spoils to the victor, that's the price of surrender. It is not for the French to re-

-sist or re - fuse.

It's come at last, it is the hour, two nations wedded in their pride: great Germany, supreme in power, and France in beauty, side by side. Somewhere tonight she be-

-trays me a - gain; flat on her back with some boy who's half her age. What can I do but hate her? With half the world in our pos - ses - sion, she still com - mands me with a glance. Un - til I'm free of this ob - ses - sion. *Spoken: I still have not defeated France.*

THE LETTER

Music by
Michel Legrand
Lyrics by
Alain Boublil/Herbert Kretzmer

you'll come to un-der-stand____ what I do, all I do,____ I do it just for you.____ Al-ways re-mem-ber:____

what I do is not my choice,

what you read is not my voice,

my love, mon a - mour.

WHAT'S LEFT OF LOVE?

Music and Lyrics by
Michel Legrand, Alain Boublil and Herbert Kretzmer

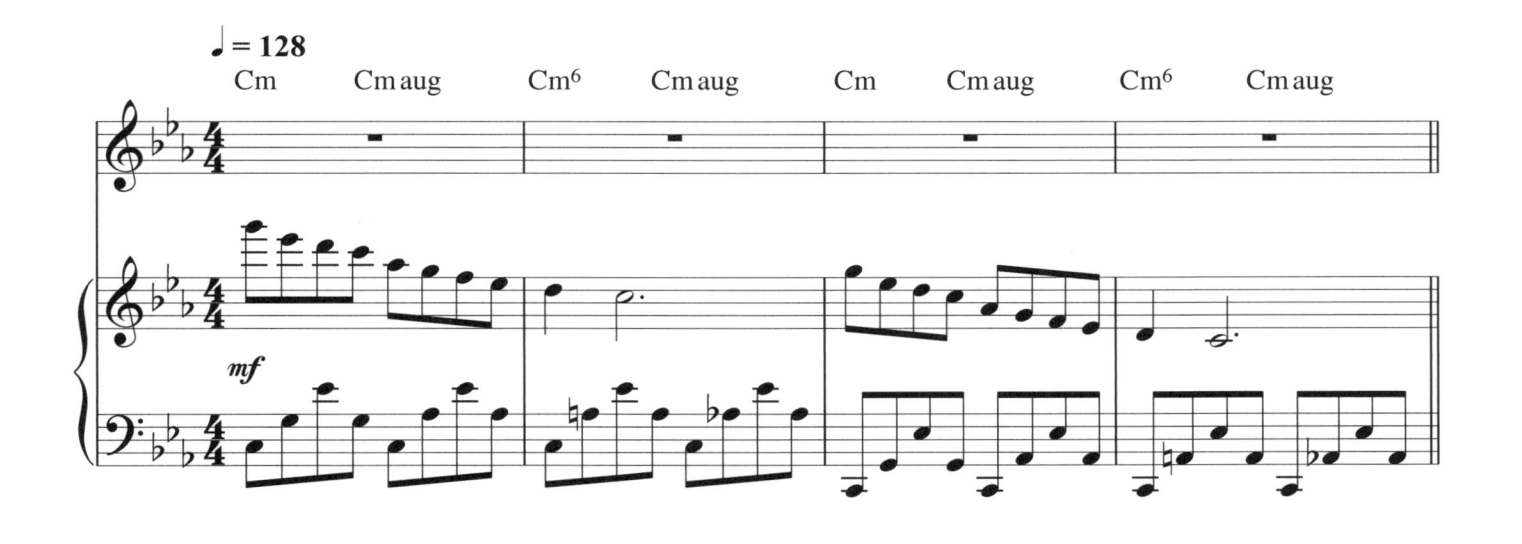

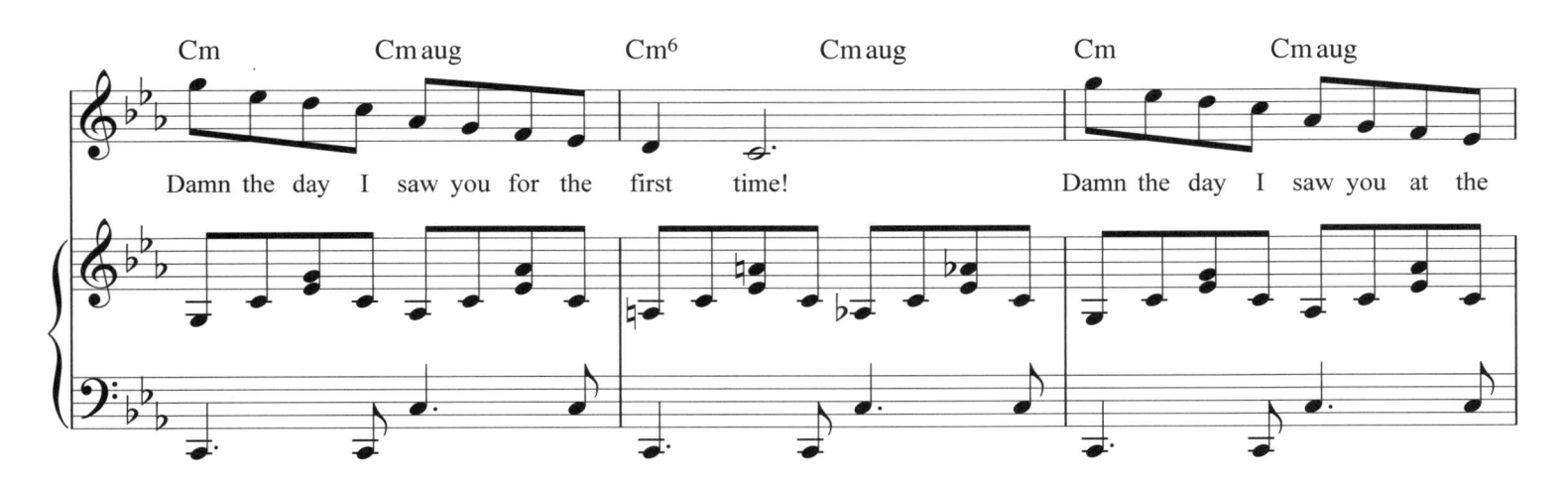

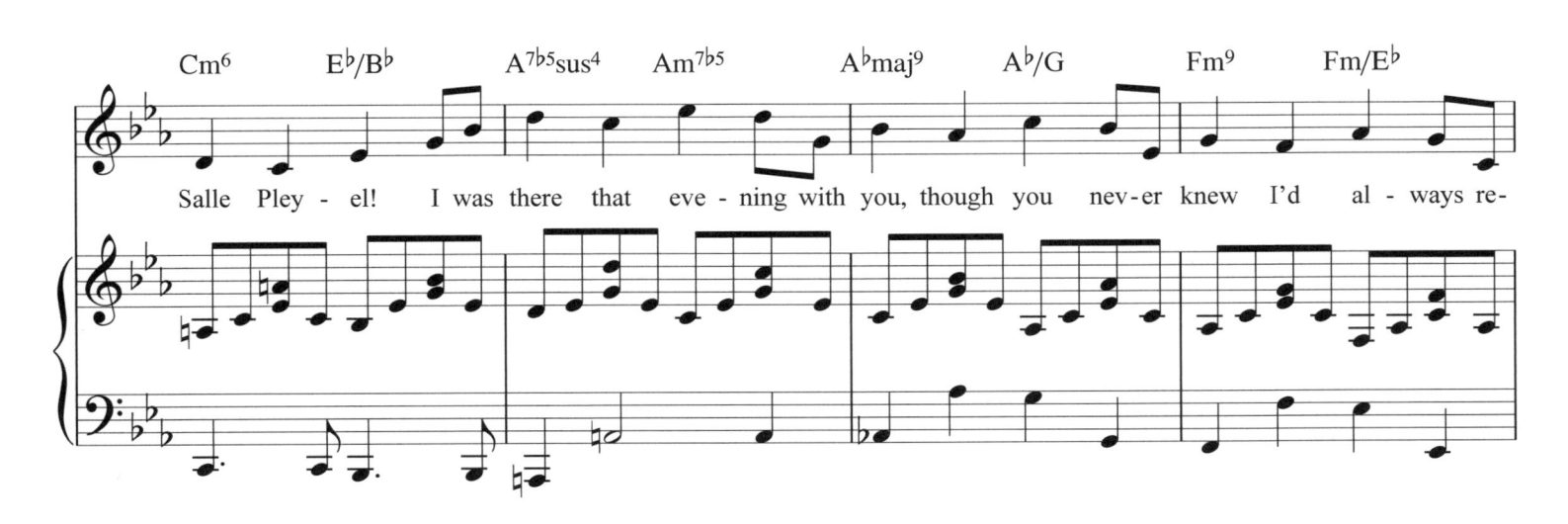

Damn the day I saw you for the first time! Damn the day I saw you at the Salle Pley-el! I was there that eve-ning with you, though you nev-er knew I'd al-ways re-

-mem - ber. Damn the day I stood there in your shad - ow, fol - low-ing your mu - sic in the Salle Pley - el! As I turned your pag - es one by one, like a flow - er turns to face the sun, so I felt my luck had just be - gun. I was thun - der - struck and

I sur - prised? Why is it strange that the chi - na doll can nev - er change? There are words that wound and words that kill; Mar - gue - rite, your words cut

lost in won - der. Must I pay for ev-'ry man who hurt you?
deep - er still! So damn the day you walked in-to my life - time!

How could I be-gin to know the price I'd pay? _____ Damn the

day! _____

poco meno mosso

Here, here in my hands, these bit - ter words that tear me a-

-part. How will I live my life? Where do I start, when each word is a knife straight to the heart? And now you shut the door, cast me a-side: a man who isn't rich, can't pro-tect, can't pro-vide. Damn your soul! Damn you! What is left of days that nev-er end-ed? What is left of all that we were

Cm6/G Cm7/G G7♭9aug N.C.
dream - ing of? What's left of
Ped.
Cm Cmaug Cm6 Cmaug Cm Cmaug
love?
Cm6 D/C D.S. al Coda
Why am
Coda
Cm Cmaug
What is left of all we felt that
Cm6 Cm7 G7♭9aug N.C. C (note only)
p
first time? What's left of love?
p
8vb

HOW DID I GET TO WHERE I AM?

Music by
Michel Legrand
Lyrics by
Alain Boublil/Herbert Kretzmer

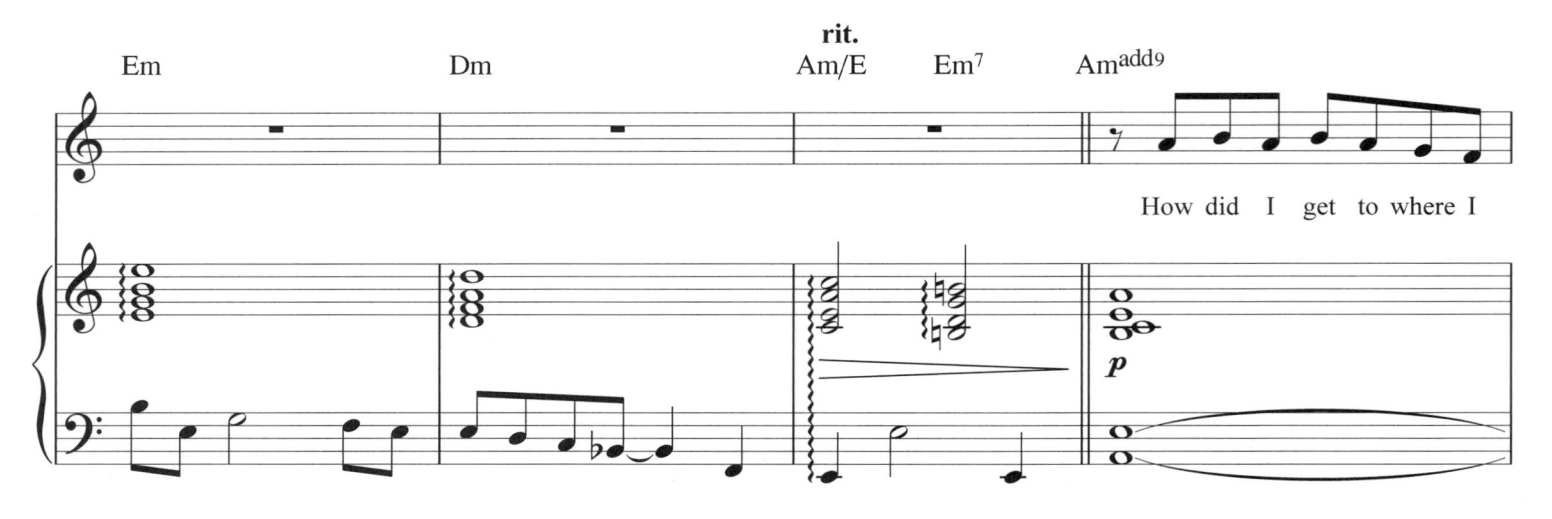

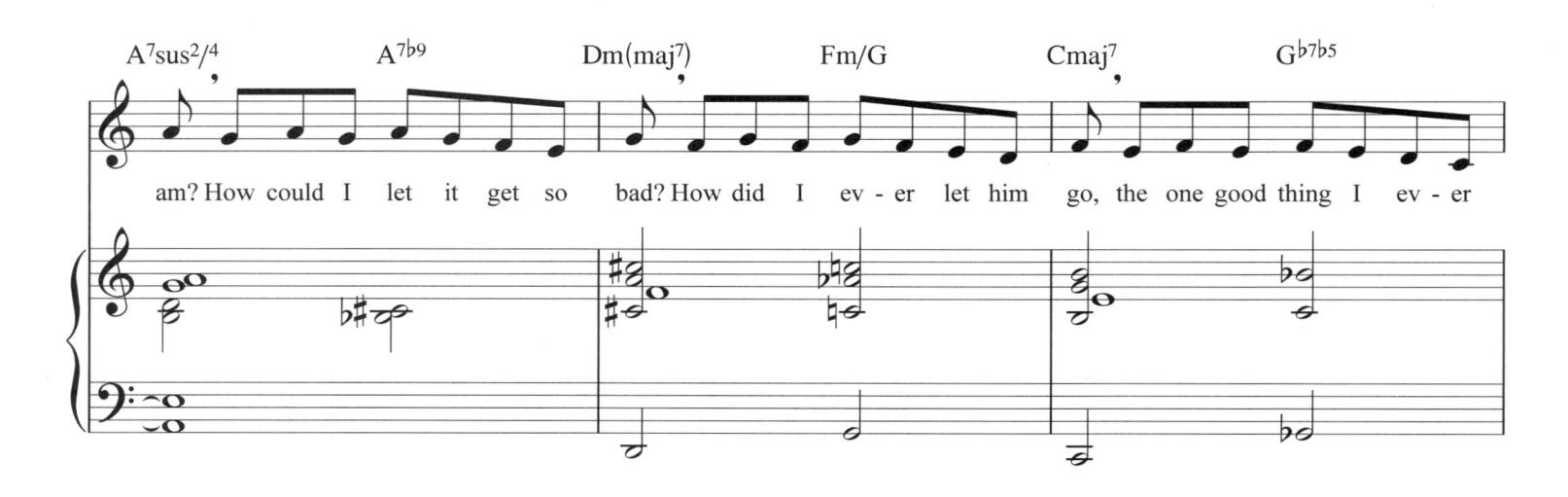

How did I get to where I am? How could I let it get so bad? How did I ever let him go, the one good thing I ever had? Why did I drift so far from home, to live my life out-side the rules, a-mong the clowns, a-mong the fools? I loved the daz-zle and the light, the sweet se-duc-tions of the night, when men of means were ev-'ry-where. They used my bed; they slept else-where. I nev-er asked what badge they wore, they left their pass-ports at the door; and ev-'ry man was just one more.

più mosso ♩ = 72

And then at last one came my way; he saw be-hind the mask I wore, he made the world seem new and gay, he saw me as a girl once

more. How did I get to where I am? How did I come to be a-lone and lose the only love I've known? He's gone, the one love I have known. With each untruth, with each mistake, I learned that time and youth don't wait, that china dolls can fall and break, that sometimes saviours come too late.

The one good thing I ever had, why did I ever let him go? How could I let it get so bad? How did I get to where I am?

FINALE

Music by
Michel Legrand
Lyrics by
Alain Boublil/Herbert Kretzmer

♩ = c.120 ma colla voce

ARMAND: Run-ning through the crowds in the town, a mil-lion peo-ple on their feet, it seemed to me ev-'ry-one was run-ning too, down ev-'ry street; and all you heard was cheer-ing. And all I thought of was to run to you.

© Copyright 2008 Bouberg Music Limited and City Lights Productions Limited.
Administered for the United Kingdom & the Republic of Ireland by Alain Boublil Overseas Limited.
Administered for the USA by Alain Boublil Music Limited (ASCAP) c/o Joel Faden & Company Incorporated.
All Rights Reserved. International Copyright Secured.

Marguerite, I promise you we'll be together now.

Marguerite, I promise you that we are free to be together; not in secret, as before. Please understand, the war is over now, and nothing now can harm you any-more. I know the sacrifice you made; I owe you more than ever can be paid.

Mar - gue - rite, this is a prom-ise I will not be-tray.

Mar - gue - rite, this is the morn-ing of a bright new day.

MARGUERITE

I've longed for this, I've prayed for this: to feel once more the kiss that changed me for al - ways. In your lov - ing eyes, now, I see what I've longed for, I see who I am. You were in my life for a moment; one brief, timeless moment. It carried me back to something I knew. The face I see I've longed to

ARMAND
Now I understand; they've told me of

see, you've come to me, and ev-'ry-thing you've done. That let-ter that you sent me was all you see is a mem-'ry. You've on-ly to save me. Mar-gue-rite, I ask you to for-give me. Mar-gue-rite, I though I was for-sa-ken. Mar-gue-

arm - our. From out of the blue, when I thought my - rite, I know I was mis - ta - ken. I'm here now. From a

poco meno mosso

life was worth noth - ing, you came and you sleep I was a - wak - ened. Now I know the rea - son why I

meno mosso

claimed me. You car - ried me back to lost you; see the sac - ri - fice, the price it cost you. It was all to

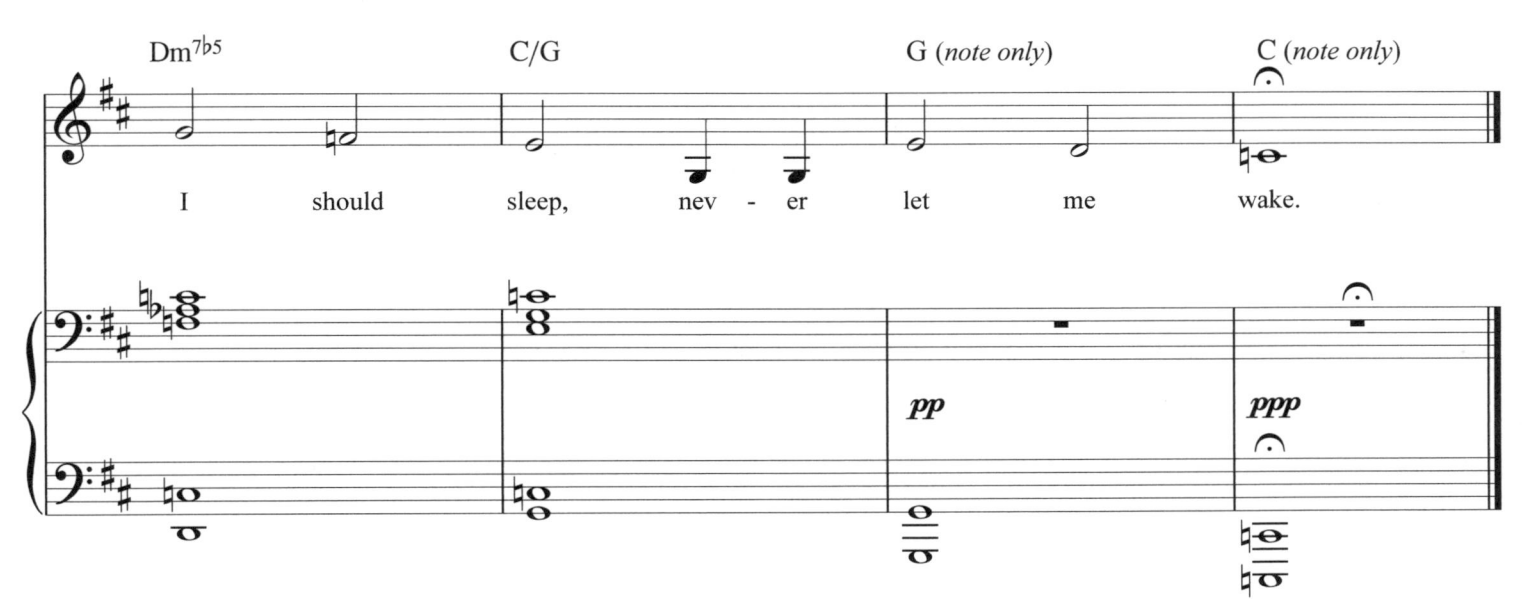

some-thing I knew. It al-ways was you. If
save me. I see it now; it al-ways was you.

molto dim.

I should fall, don't let me break. If

I should sleep, nev-er let me wake.

pp *ppp*

All songs in this edition © 2008
Bouberg Music Limited/City Lights Productions Limited,
Alain Boublil Music Limited Administrator (ASCAP)

Non-Dramatic and Performance Rights
administered for the United Kingdom by
Alain Boublil Overseas Limited (PRS)
c/o 62a Pont Street Mews, London SW1X 0AF,
e-mail: sue@abol.co.uk

and in the rest of the world by
Alain Boublil Music Limited (ASCAP)
c/o Joel Faden & Company, Inc.,
1775 Broadway, New York, NY 10019, USA,
e-mail: mwlock@joelfaden.com

Copyright Dramatic Performance Rights
controlled and licensed by
Bouberg Productions Limited
c/o MBST Entertainment, Inc.,
345 North Maple Drive, Beverly Hills, CA 90210, USA,
e-mail: stevet@mbst.com

Published by:
Wise Publications,
14-15 Berners Street, London W1T 3LJ, UK.

Exclusive Distributors:
Music Sales Limited,
Distribution Centre, Newmarket Road,
Bury St. Edmunds, Suffolk IP33 3YB, UK.
Music Sales Pty Limited,
20 Resolution Drive, Caringbah, NSW 2229, Australia.

Order No. AM995500
ISBN 978-1-84772-741-1
This book © Copyright 2008 by Wise Publications,
a division of Music Sales Limited.

Unauthorised reproduction of any part of this publication
by any means including photocopying is an infringement of copyright.

Music arranged by Jack Long.
Music processed by Paul Ewers Music Design.
Edited by Fiona Bolton.

Printed in the EU.

Your Guarantee of Quality
As publishers, we strive to produce every book
to the highest commercial standards.
The music has been freshly engraved and the book
has been carefully designed to minimise awkward
page turns and to make playing from it a real pleasure.
Particular care has been given to specifying acid-free, neutral-sized paper
made from pulps which have not been elemental chlorine bleached.
This pulp is from farmed sustainable forests and was
produced with special regard for the environment.
Throughout, the printing and binding have been planned to ensure
a sturdy, attractive publication which should give years of enjoyment.
If your copy fails to meet our high standards, please inform us
and we will gladly replace it.

www.musicsales.com